This item is no longer property
of Pima County Public Library
Sale of this item benefited the Library

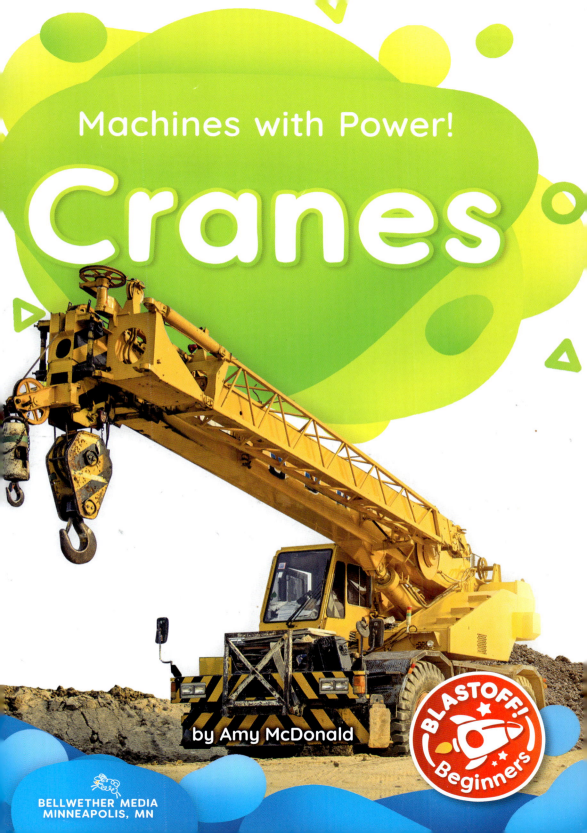

Blastoff! Beginners are developed by literacy experts and educators to meet the needs of early readers. These engaging informational texts support young children as they begin reading about their world. Through simple language and high frequency words paired with crisp, colorful photos, Blastoff! Beginners launch young readers into the universe of independent reading.

Sight Words in This Book

a	from	on	they
and	help	out	this
are	here	see	to
big	is	sit	up
can	it	the	water
down	look	there	you

This edition first published in 2021 by Bellwether Media, Inc.

No part of this publication may be reproduced in whole or in part without written permission of the publisher. For information regarding permission, write to Bellwether Media, Inc., Attention: Permissions Department, 6012 Blue Circle Drive, Minnetonka, MN 55343.

Library of Congress Cataloging-in-Publication Data

Names: McDonald, Amy, 1985- author.
Title: Cranes / by Amy McDonald.
Description: Minneapolis, MN : Bellwether Media, Inc., 2021. | Series: Blastoff! Beginners : Machines with power! | Includes bibliographical references and index. | Audience: Ages PreK-2 | Audience: Grades K-1
Identifiers: LCCN 2020029230 (print) | LCCN 2020029231 (ebook) | ISBN 9781644873687 | ISBN 9781648340697 (ebook)
Subjects: LCSH: Cranes, derricks, etc.--Juvenile literature.
Classification: LCC TJ1363 .M29 2021 (print) | LCC TJ1363 (ebook) | DDC 621.8/73--dc23
LC record available at https://lccn.loc.gov/2020029230
LC ebook record available at https://lccn.loc.gov/2020029231

Text copyright © 2021 by Bellwether Media, Inc. BLASTOFF! BEGINNERS and associated logos are trademarks and/or registered trademarks of Bellwether Media, Inc.

Editor: Christina Leaf   Designer: Andrea Schneider

Printed in the United States of America, North Mankato, MN.

Table of Contents

What Are Cranes?	4
Parts of a Crane	8
Cranes at Work	16
Crane Facts	22
Glossary	23
To Learn More	24
Index	24

What Are Cranes?

Look up!
Can you see
the crane?

Cranes are tall machines. They lift and move big **loads**.

loads

Parts of a Crane

This is the **boom**. It goes up and down.

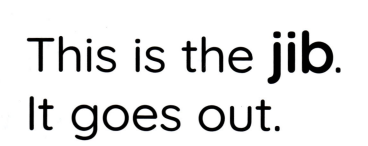

This is the **jib**.
It goes out.

This is the hook.
It holds the load.

This is the **cab**.
The driver sits here.

Cranes at Work

This crane sits on water. It helps build a bridge.

This is a crane truck. It moves from place to place.

This is a tower crane. It does work up high. Hello up there!

Crane Facts

Crane Parts

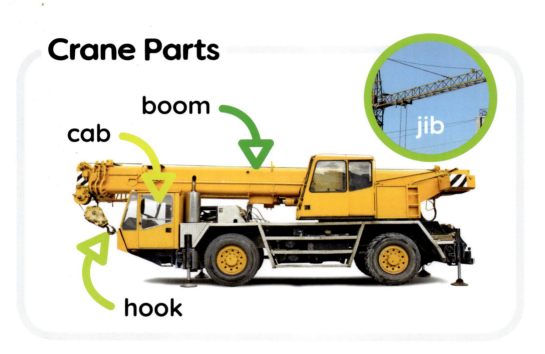

cab
boom
hook
jib

Types of Cranes

floating crane

crane truck

tower crane

Glossary

boom

the part of a crane that moves things up and down

cab

a place where the driver sits

jib

the arm on some cranes that reaches out

loads

things that are lifted

To Learn More

ON THE WEB

FACTSURFER

Factsurfer.com gives you a safe, fun way to find more information.

1. Go to www.factsurfer.com.

2. Enter "cranes" into the search box and click 🔍.

3. Select your book cover to see a list of related content.

Index

boom, 8, 9
bridge, 16
build, 16
cab, 14, 15
crane truck, 18
driver, 14
holds, 12
hook, 12, 13
jib, 10, 11

lift, 6
loads, 6, 12
machines, 6
move, 6, 18
sits, 14, 16
tower crane, 20
water, 16
work, 20

The images in this book are reproduced through the courtesy of: Bannafarsai_Stock, front cover; Lalocracio, p. 3; gyn9037, pp. 4-5; Roman023_photography, p. 6 (loads); ZoranOrcik, pp. 6-7, 23 (boom); Dmitry Kalinovsky, pp. 8-9, 18-19; Bigpra, pp. 10-11; Zuberka, pp. 12-13; kozmoat98, pp. 14-15; ollo, pp. 16-17; Sergei Dubrovskii, pp. 20-21; Blade_kostas, p. 22 (parts); LM3311, p. 22 (jib); AM Stock 2/ Alamy, p. 22 (floating crane); evgenii mitroshin, p. 22 (crane truck); Bullstar, p. 22 (tower crane); Praphan Jampala, p. 23 (cab); Pavlo Lys, p. 23 (jib); AlexKZ, p. 23 (loads).